MEDICAL DETECTIVE DOGS

by Frances E. Ruffin

Consultant: Wilma Melville, Founder
National Disaster Search Dog Foundation

New York, New York

Special thanks to Wilma Melville who founded the:
National Disaster Search Dog Foundation
206 N. Signal Street, Suite R
Ojai, CA 93023
(888) 4K9-HERO
www.SearchDogFoundation.org

The Search Dog Foundation is a not-for-profit organization that rescues dogs, gives them professional training, and partners them with firefighters to find people buried alive in disasters. They produce the most highly trained search dogs in the nation.

To Juanita and Arthur Harland

Credits

Cover and Title Page, courtesy of Dianne & Jim Walker; Cover (RT), courtesy of Dianne & Jim Walker; Cover (RM), © Frank Anderson, Lexington Herald-Leader / AP Images; Cover (RB), courtesy of Slade Mead; TOC, © Bonnie Weller, Philadelphia Inquirer; 4, courtesy of Gillian Lacey & Passionate Productions (UK); 5(T), courtesy of Gillian Lacey & Passionate Productions (UK); 5(B), courtesy of Gillian Lacey & Passionate Productions (UK); 6, courtesy of Dianne & Jim Walker; 7, courtesy of Dianne & Jim Walker; 8, courtesy of Dianne & Jim Walker; 9, courtesy of Dianne & Jim Walker; 10–11, © San Francisco Chronicle; 11, © San Francisco Chronicle; 12, © Robert Tong, Marin Independent Journal; 13, © Jim Gensheimer, San Jose Mercury News. Copyright San Jose Mercury News. All rights reserved; 14, © Mary Beth Taylor; 15, courtesy of Slade Mead; 16–17, © Mary Beth Taylor; 17, © Mary Beth Taylor; 18, © Bonnie Weller, Philadelphia Inquirer; 18–19, courtesy of Kevin Weaver; 20, courtesy of Elizabeth Sparacino and Matthew Sparacino; 21, © Frank Anderson, Lexington Herald-Leader / AP Images; 22, © Joy Powers, Photos by Joy; 23, courtesy of Great Plains Assistance Dogs Foundation; 24–25, © Joy Powers, Photos by Joy; 25, © Joy Powers, Photos by Joy; 26, © Mary Beth Taylor; 27, courtesy of Dianne & Jim Walker; 28(TL), © Tim Davis / Photo Researchers, Inc.; 28(TR), © John Daniels / Ardea; 28(BL), © John Daniels / Ardea; 28(BR), © Photodisc / Fotosearch.com.

Publisher: Kenn Goin
Project Editor: Lisa Wiseman
Creative Director: Spencer Brinker
Photo Researcher: Amy Dunleavy
Original Design: Dawn Beard Creative

Library of Congress Cataloging-in-Publication Data

Ruffin, Frances E.
  Medical detectives dogs / by Frances E. Ruffin.
    p. cm. — (Dog heroes)
  Includes bibliographical references and index.
  ISBN-13: 978-1-59716-251-7 (library binding)
  ISBN-10: 1-59716-251-5 (library binding)
  ISBN-13: 978-1-59716-279-1 (pbk.)
  ISBN-10: 1-59716-279-5 (pbk.)
 1. Detector dogs—Juvenile literature. 2. Medical emergencies
—Prevention—Juvenile literature. I. Title. II. Series.

RC86.5.R84 2007
636.73—dc22

                    2006012210

For more information, write to Bearport Publishing Company, Inc., 101 Fifth Avenue, Suite 6R, New York, New York 10003. Printed in the United States of America.

10 9 8 7 6 5 4 3 2 1

Table of Contents

Man's Best Friend

Trudii, a Dalmatian, walked toward her owner, Gillian Lacey. Suddenly, the dog stopped and began to sniff and then lick Gillian's leg. Gillian wondered if she had spilled something on herself. She looked down, but there was nothing there except for a tiny mole on her leg.

Trudii

For the next six months Trudii kept sniffing and licking the same spot on Gillian's leg. Finally, Gillian decided to see a doctor, who discovered that the mole was **melanoma**. The doctor told her that she had to have an operation. This deadly form of skin **cancer** needed to be removed. Trudii had saved Gillian's life.

When Gillian got home from the hospital, Trudii proved that the cancer was gone. She no longer sniffed and licked Gillian's leg.

Gillian's leg after the operation

Gillian Lacey

Saving Lives

In the United States and England, some dogs are being trained to become medical **detectives**. They're helping scientists find cancer in people. How are dogs able to detect this disease?

Dianne and Jim Walker with Stormy

Dogs have a much stronger sense of smell than humans. Some scientists believe that many diseases give off **scents** that dogs can smell. Scientists are working on **experiments** with these animals to prove that this idea is true.

Dr. James Walker and his wife, Dianne, run a **laboratory** at Florida State University. There, they're working with Stormy, a standard schnauzer. They performed a test with Stormy to find out if he can detect cancer by smell.

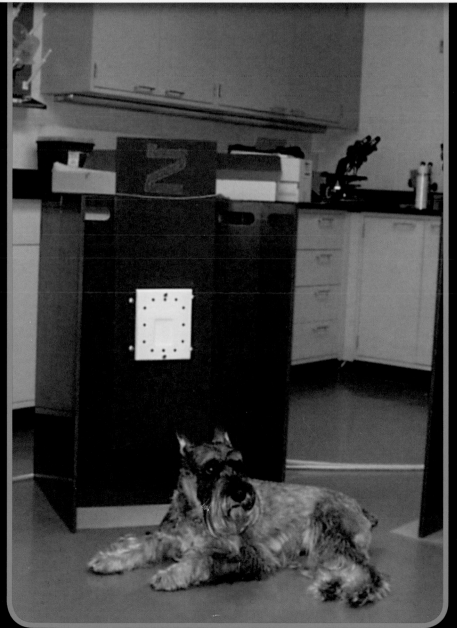

In a study, Dr. Walker proved that a dog's sense of smell is 10,000 to 100,000 times better than a human's.

Stormy in the laboratory

Stormy the Detective

During the test, Stormy had to find and retrieve items that had a certain smell. First, Dianne took five tubes and drilled small holes in each one. In one of the tubes she put in a **chemical** called n-Amyl Acetate, which smells like bananas. Dianne let Stormy smell it. "Amyl," she said to him.

Stormy sniffing the
n-Amyl Acetate

Dianne scattered the tubes, which all looked alike, in a grassy area outdoors. Then she told Stormy to find the one with the chemical. When Stormy brought back the right tube, Dianne hugged him and said, "Good boy!"

The results of Stormy's test showed that he is well trained, has a good sense of smell, and may be able to detect diseases.

Stormy brings the tube with the n-Amyl Acetate to Dianne.

Pine Street Foundation

Pine Street Foundation is another laboratory working with dogs to see if they can detect cancer. Three Labrador retrievers and two Portuguese Water Dogs took part in Pine Street's experiment.

In 2003, Ling Tan (left) and Ming Shing (right) were trained to become medical detective dogs at Pine Street.

The dogs, ages 7 to 18 months, all had puppy training. They were picked because they were eager to sniff things and listen to commands. The animals went through a tough but short training program. They were taught to sniff tubes to find the ones that held breath samples from cancer patients. The dogs got a food reward every time they found the right smell.

Kirk Turner, a dog trainer, rewards Ling Tan and Ming Shing with food.

Scientists have used different dog breeds in their experiments to detect human cancer.

Experiments

After the training was over, the experiment was ready to start. Scientists asked 86 cancer patients and 83 healthy people to breathe into tubes. These were not the same people whose breath samples were used in the training program. The dogs had never smelled these samples before.

Isabell was one of the first dogs taught to sniff out cancer at Pine Street.

Then the dogs were led into a room filled with the tubes. When they found breath from a cancer patient, they sat or lay down in front of the sample. More than 12,200 tests were done. Depending on the type of cancer, the dogs found the patients' samples 88 to 99 percent of the time.

A dog's ability to detect cancer is still being studied. If a person feels sick, he or she should always talk with a doctor to find out what's wrong.

Kobi, another dog at Pine Street, demonstrating his cancer-detecting abilities

Gracie Love

Other dogs have become different kinds of medical detectives. Wherever Lindsay Mead goes, her dog Gracie Love is not far behind. In fact, Gracie, a yellow Labrador retriever, is right by her side. She is much more than a pet. Gracie is trained to warn Lindsay whenever she senses that Lindsay is about to have a **seizure**.

Lindsay and Gracie Love

Lindsay has **epilepsy**. People who have this disease can suddenly lose **consciousness** and fall down. When this happens, they may hurt themselves or not know what happened when they wake up. During falls, Lindsay has broken bones and even lost teeth.

More than 2.7 million people in the United States have epilepsy.

Gracie Love with a treat

Into Action

Some people with epilepsy know when they're about to have a seizure. They can lie down before it starts. However, since Lindsay doesn't know beforehand, Gracie has to watch her. When she senses that Lindsay is about to have trouble, she **alerts** her to the problem.

Gracie demonstrates how she alerts Lindsay to a seizure.

Gracie pulls a cord on a small **alarm** that Lindsay wears on her belt. When Lindsay hears the alarm, she sits or lies down so that she won't fall. The alarm also lets Lindsay's parents, teachers, and friends know that she needs help. After pulling the cord, Gracie snuggles up with Lindsay. When she comes out of her seizure, Lindsay feels safe and calm.

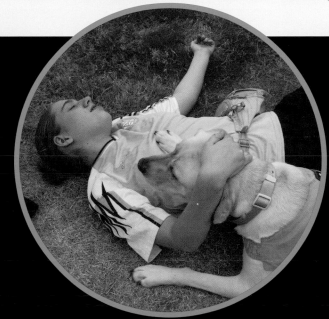

Gracie demonstrates how she stays close to Lindsay until she wakes up from her seizure.

By staying calm, Gracie lets others know that Lindsay will be all right.

17

Help Is on the Way

Gracie is one of many dogs that can help people who have certain diseases. Some dogs are trained to tell when their owners are going to pass out from **diabetes**.

Chewie goes food shopping with his owner Bob, who has diabetes. Chewie can detect when Bob might pass out.

Dogs that help people who have epilepsy or diabetes have many different names. They are known as seizure-assist dogs, medical assistance dogs, or emergency medical response dogs.

A beagle named Belle knew that her owner, Kevin Weaver, was becoming very sick. Kevin, who has diabetes, began to pass out. As she was taught to do, Belle found Kevin's cell phone and bit down on the number 9. This number is programmed to call 911. Then she barked into the phone. In a short time, an ambulance was at the house. Belle, also known as Belle the Wonder Dog, had saved Kevin's life.

Kevin Weaver and Belle

Super Noses?

Scientists aren't sure how dogs know when their owners are about to have medical trouble. However, they have some ideas. Some people believe that a sick person gives off a scent that only a dog can smell.

Others feel that dogs are good detectives because of the strong **bond** between pets and humans. Due to this close friendship, dogs notice the smallest changes in the way their owners act. They are able to sense when these changes mean their owners need their help.

Cheyenne, age seven, and her dog, Mikki, are best friends. Mikki is able to help Cheyenne when she has an epileptic seizure.

Dogs can usually alert people about attacks seconds or minutes before they happen. Sometimes they have even warned people as long as 12 hours before a seizure takes place.

Training

No matter how they do it, these amazing detective dogs and their owners need special training. That's why Lindsay Mead and her dad traveled to the tiny town of Jud, North Dakota. There, at the Great Plains Assistance Dogs Foundation, Gracie was born and trained as a seizure-assist dog.

Great Plains Assistance Dogs Foundation

701-685-2242

● SERVICE DOGS ● SPECIALTY DOGS ● HEARING DOGS
● THERAPEUTIC DOGS ● SEIZURE RESPONSE RESEARCH

Dogs are not the only animals being trained to sniff out disease in humans. In Africa, giant pouched rats are trained to detect tuberculosis, a lung disease.

The puppies chosen for the foundation's training program must be able to work in public places. They need to be well behaved and understand what is going on around them.

When they first come into the program, the pups go through basic training. Then, at 18 to 20 months, they begin to learn how to work with people who have epilepsy or diabetes.

Puppies at Great Plains

Becoming a Team

When Lindsay got to the foundation, she first worked with a trained dog. She was taught how to give important commands, such as *Sit* and *Come*. Learning this would help her become "the leader" when she got her own dog.

Travis demonstrates how a student at Great Plains learns to give commands to a dog. Here he is telling Beamer to stay.

When Lindsay finally met Gracie, they quickly became friends. The pair trained for several hours a day for three weeks. First, they learned how to work together as a team. Then, Gracie learned how to alert and care for Lindsay before, during, and after a seizure.

Blazer, a black Labrador retriever, licks Travis to demonstrate how he would care for the boy during a seizure.

Some dogs alert by whining, barking, or pawing at a person's clothes. Then the dog stands or lies beside his or her owner until the seizure is over.

Medical Heroes

Dogs such as Gracie help their owners become more **independent**. With Gracie by her side, Lindsay doesn't have to worry about being alone when she has a seizure. These animals help their owners lead regular lives.

Gracie and Lindsay practice soccer together. Gracie even has her own uniform!

Using dogs to find cancer is still in an experimental stage. However, as scientists learn more about the animals' abilities in this area, they believe even more lives will be saved.

Most of the dogs who help people with medical problems are pets as well as detectives. To the people whose lives they save, however, they are also heroes.

Some scientists hope to create a computer "nose." This tool would be able to detect diseases without the use of a dog.

Stormy

Just the Facts

- By law, people are allowed to bring their seizure-assist dogs into public places such as stores and theaters.

- People may pay from $8,000 to $15,000 for a trained medical assistance dog. There are groups, however, that can help people who don't have the money to buy one.

- Bill Burns of Indiana has diabetes. One night he passed out in a cornfield. He needed his medicine right away. Lucky for him, his dogs, Dusty and Butch, were there. Dusty lay across Bill to keep him warm. Butch held Bill's flashlight in his mouth. A policeman who was driving by saw the light and took Bill to the hospital.

- Nancy Best thinks that Mia, her yellow Labrador retriever, is a real lifesaver. About six years ago, Nancy noticed that Mia kept sniffing at the same spot on her body. She decided to go to the doctor. It was lucky for Nancy that she did. Her doctors found a **tumor** and operated right away. Now, Nancy is cancer-free.

- In 2006, Belle the beagle received an award for saving the life of her owner—Kevin Weaver.

Medical Detective Dogs

beagle

standard schnauzer

Portuguese Water Dog

Labrador retriever

alarm (uh-LARM) something with a bell or buzzer that warns people of danger

alerts (uh-LURTS) gives a warning

bond (BOND) a close friendship or connection with someone

cancer (KAN-sur) a serious, sometimes fatal disease that destroys parts of the body

chemical (KEM-uh-kuhl) a natural or man-made substance

consciousness (KON-shuhss-ness) to be awake and aware

detectives (di-TEK-tivz) people or animals that solve mysteries

diabetes (*dye*-uh-BEE-teez) a disease in which a person has too much sugar in his or her blood; can cause a person to pass out

epilepsy (EP-uh-*lep*-see) a brain disease that can cause seizures

experiments (ek-SPER-uh-ments) tests to figure out if an idea is true

independent (*in*-di-PEN-duhnt) able to do things without help

laboratory (LAB-ruh-*tor*-ee) a place to test experiments

melanoma (*mel*-uh-NOH-muh) a dangerous and sometimes deadly form of skin cancer

scents (SENTS) the smells people or animals give off

seizure (SEE-zhur) a sudden attack that can cause a person to shake and even lose consciousness

tumor (TOO-mur) an unusual lump or growth in the body

Bibliography

Dalziel, Deborah, and Sharon Hermansen. *Service Dogs for People with Seizure Disorders: An Informational Guide.* Gainesville, FL (2000).

Davis, Joel. *With Alex by My Side.* Laceyville, PA: Toad Hall Press (2000).

Dibsie, Patricia. *Love Heels: Tales from Canine Companions for Independence.* New York: Yorkville Press (2003).

Lingenfelter, Mike, and David Frei. *The Angel by My Side: The True Story of a Dog Who Saved a Man . . . and a Man Who Saved a Dog.* Carlsbad, CA: Hay House (2002).

Read More

George, Jean Craighead. *How to Talk to Your Dog.* New York: HarperCollins (2000).

Grace, Catherine O'Neill. *Dogs on Duty.* Washington, D.C.: National Geographic Society (1988).

Kent, Deborah. *Animal Helpers for the Disabled.* Danbury, CT: Franklin Watts (2003).

Singer, Marilyn. *A Dog's Gotta Do What a Dog's Gotta Do: Dogs at Work.* New York: Henry Holt (2000).

Learn More Online

Visit these Web sites to learn more about medical assistance dogs, epilepsy, and medical detective dogs:

www.caninecompanions.org/

www.epilepsyfoundation.org/kidsclub/nonflash/home/index.html

www.i-love-dogs.com/dogsarticles/Medical-Dogs.html

Index

About the Author

Frances E. Ruffin is a writer who lives in New York City. She has written
24 nonfiction books for children. This is her fourth book about dog heroes.